THE FRUIT CALLED LOVE

This book belongs to:

....

But the fruit of the Spirit is love...

Galatians 5:22

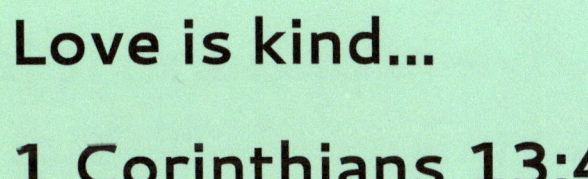

Love is kind...

1 Corinthians 13:4

Love means doing nice things for others

...even on days when we don't feel like it!

...Love is patient, it is not self-seeking

1 Corinthians 13:4

Love is caring, sharing and being considerate with others.

Love is being patient with others at the play ground ...taking turns as we play.

Love is caring for our environment

Love always protect

1 Corinthians 13:7

No one has seen God; but if we love one another, God lives in us and his love is made complete in us.

1 John 4:12

Love is being concerned about those in the neighborhood.

"Be kind to one another, tenderhearted, forgiving one another as God in Christ forgave you."

Ephesians 4:32

"It means being nice to your friends at school."

Love is being kind to your siblings.

My command is this: Love each other as I have loved you.

John 15:12

Love is being obedient to your parent and doing things that make them happy.

Children, obey your parent in the lord for this is right

Ephesians 6:1

Love does not dishonor others.

1 Corinthians 13:5

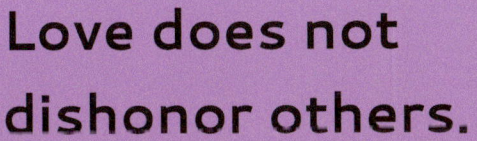

Honor your father and mother." This is the first commandment with a promise...

Ephesians 6:2

Love means stopping someone from hurting others.

Love does not delight in evil but rejoices with the truth.

1 Corinthians 13:6

Carry each other's burdens, and in this way you will fulfill the law of Christ.

Galatians 6:2

Love means giving a hug of comfort and showing that you care.

Love means treating everyone equally irrespective of race, gender, abilities and character.

Keep on loving one another as brothers and sisters

Hebrew 13:1

On our own, our ability to love is limited, but through Christ, we are able to love effortlessly because we know God who is love.

1 John 4:7

WRITTEN BY
ANTHONIA UDEMEH

www.ingramcontent.com/pod-product-compliance
Lightning Source LLC
Chambersburg PA
CBHW040024130526
44590CB00036B/88